First Nature B

The Worm

Gunilla Ingves

A & C Black · London

A & C Black (Publishers) Ltd, 35 Bedford Row,
London WC1R 4JH
First published by Natur och Kultur, Sweden under the series title *Har du sett på...*

Translated by Jane Sutton
Nature advisor English text, Jean Imrie

Ingves, Gunilla
Worm. — (First nature books)
1. The Worm — Juvenile literature
I. Title II. Daggmasken. *English*
III. Series
595.1 QL386
ISBN 0-7136-2649-6

ISBN 0-7136-2649-6

This edition arranged with the help of Angus Hudson, London
Printed and bound in Great Britain by Purnell and Son (Book Production) Ltd., Paulton, Bristol

Down in the ground a worm is burrowing its way
through the earth.

Close by, another worm is tunnelling in the earth. These two worms are going to mate, so that they can have young worms.

Both worms have eggs and sperm inside their bodies. They need to swap sperm so that their eggs will be fertilised. Then young worms can start to grow inside the eggs. The two worms lie close together, head to tail and swap sperm.

When they have finished mating, a sticky fluid oozes out of the fat part of each worm. The eggs and sperm are inside the fluid.

Now the worms wriggle out of the fluid and the fluid turns to jelly.

Inside the jelly, the eggs and sperm mix together. The sperm fertilises the eggs. Soon young worms grow inside the eggs.

One day, an egg hatches.
A tiny worm crawls out of
the egg.

Then it wriggles out of the
jelly.

The worm's body is made up of lots of segments. The biggest segment is called the saddle. This young worm won't grow a saddle until it is a year old.

The worm doesn't have any eyes, so it can't see. But it can sense the sunlight through its skin. It doesn't have any ears either, so it can't hear. But it can tell if anything is moving nearby.

As soon as the worm hatches, it starts to burrow through the earth. It moves along by squashing up its back end and stretching out its front end. The worm hasn't got any legs, but it has four pairs of bristles on each segment of its body. The bristles help it grip the earth as it moves along.

Sometimes the ground is hard and the worm has to eat its way through the earth. All the goodness in the earth is used for food. The worm passes the rest out at the back. It churns up the earth as it goes along.

At night, the worm comes up out of its tunnels. It is cool and damp on the ground. The worm drinks some dew from a leaf.

The worm finds some food on the ground. It eats small bits of dead leaves and roots and takes some back to its food store. But now the worm has to hurry because a flea beetle is coming. The flea beetle likes to eat worms.

Centipedes eat worms too. The worm has to escape, so it crawls up out of the ground into the sunlight.

It is too hot for the worm to stay on top of the ground.
If the worm's skin dries out, it won't be able to breathe.
It finds another tunnel to hide in.

Soon it starts to rain and the tunnels begin to fill with water. The worm has to come up to the top of the ground again.

One poor worm is stuck in a puddle. It musn't stay under water too long or it won't be able to breathe.

When the rain stops, the worm starts burrowing again. It churns up the earth, letting air and water get into the ground. Sometimes it pulls dead leaves down into the ground. All this helps the plants in the garden to grow.

Now it is autumn and someone is digging the garden. Suddenly, a spade chops the worm in two.

A little girl finds the worm. She feels sad, but the worm will be all right. It can grow a new tail end.

When the garden has been dug, the little girl rakes up some leaves that have fallen from a tree. She puts all the leaves in a big basket.

She tips the leaves onto the garden. Now the worm will have plenty of food. The leaves will also help to keep the earth warm in the cold weather.

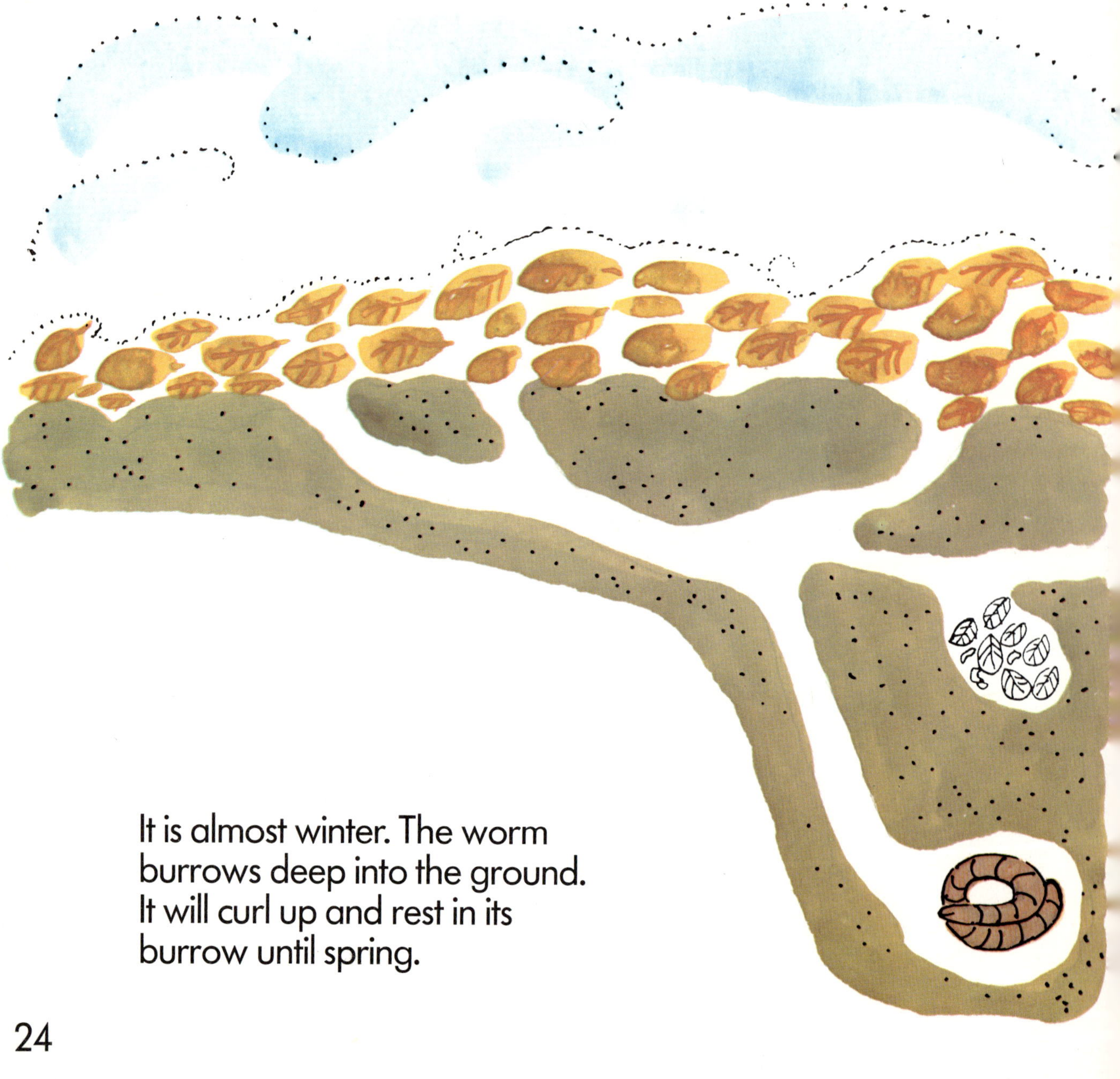

It is almost winter. The worm burrows deep into the ground. It will curl up and rest in its burrow until spring.